Ocean

Susan Canizares • Pamela Chanko

Scholastic Inc.
New York • Toronto • London • Auckland • Sydney

Acknowledgments

Science Consultants: Patrick R. Thomas, Ph.D., Bronx Zoo/Wildlife Conservation Park; Glenn Phillips, The New York Botanical Garden
Literacy Specialist: Ada Cordova, District 2, New York City

Design: MKR Design, Inc.

Photo Research: Barbara Scott

Endnotes: Susan Russell

Endnote Illustrations: Craig Spearing

Photographs: Cover: M.C. Chamberlain/DRK Photo; p. 1: E. R. Degginger/Photo Researchers; p. 2: F. Stuart Westmorland/Photo Researchers; p. 3: Mark Newman/Photo Researchers; p. 4: David Hall/Photo Researchers; p. 5: Jeff Rotman/Jeff Rotman Photography; p. 6: Tom Bean/DRK Photo; p. 7: Donna McLaughlin/The Stock Market; p. 8: Tom Bean/DRK Photo; p. 9: David Hall/Photo Researchers; p. 10: Nancy Rotenberg/Animals, Animals; p. 11: T.A. Wiewandt/DRK Photo; p. 12: Tom & Therisa Stack/Tom Stack Assoc.

Library of Congress Cataloging-in-Publication Data
Canizares, Susan
Ocean / Susan Canizares, Pamela Chanko.
p. cm. -- (Science emergent readers)
Includes index.
Summary: Photographs and simple text introduce the ocean
environment and what is found in it.
ISBN 0-590-63886-6 (pbk.: alk. paper)
1. Oceanography--Juvenile literature.   2. Marine biology--Juvenile literature. [1. Ocean.]
I. Chanko, Pamela, 1968-.   II. Title.   III. Series
GC21.5.C24   1998
551.46--dc21   98-23226
CIP AC

20 19   08   06 07 08 9/0

The ocean.

The ocean has water

and waves.

The ocean has plants

and animals.

The ocean has rocks

and sand.

The ocean has coral

and fish.

The ocean has shells,

fossils, and sometimes...

hidden treasure!

Ocean

Three quarters of our planet is covered by four oceans. The Pacific Ocean is the largest. Next is the Atlantic, then the Indian, and then the Arctic. Along with the smaller seas and gulfs, they create an interlaced system that spreads over the entire earth. We depend on the oceans for so many things that life could not exist without them.

Oceans are made up of saltwater, but we get all our water from them. Ocean water evaporates, loses its heavy salts, and rises up into the air to form clouds. Then it falls back down onto the earth as rain, which is the freshwater that we drink. It nourishes all the plants, animals, and people of our planet.

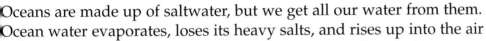

Waves are formed by several forces. We see waves that the wind makes when it blows across the water, but much of the movement of the water is from the tides that are caused by the moon's gravitational pull.

Plants and animals are part of the vast marine life of the oceans. Many plants thrive under the water, just as others do on land, providing food and shelter for many species. The dissolved oxygen that plants produce is what the underwater creatures breathe. But mammals that breathe air also call the ocean their home. Some of the best known are porpoises, dolphins, and whales.

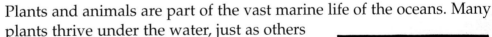

Long ago, people thought that the bottom of the ocean was flat and made out of sand. Now we know that the ocean floor is like the land, with rocks, mountains, valleys, and high cliffs. The sand that we see on the beaches is created by the surf constantly pounding rocks into tiny

bits. The sands of the oceans are always on the move, deposited by high tides and then taken out to sea again at low tide.

In some parts of the ocean, there are huge beds of coral that have formed over many years. Coral is made of the skeletons of tiny ocean organisms that build up on top of each other. It forms the architecture that plants grow on and that many forms of sealife use for homes and hiding places.

Fish far outnumber any other kind of marine life in the ocean. There are over 20,000 species. They are usually colored to match the waters they live in, and their shapes are perfect for their lives of swimming.

Shells belong to the order of mollusca. They are the outside coverings of the soft-bodied creatures that lived inside. Shells are created when fluid

secreted by the creatures' bodies hardens. It works like concrete, but faster. Fossils are the impressions of plants and animals in clay or other soft material that has become rock over millions of years. Fossils help us know what life in the ocean was like long, long ago.

The oceans have many secrets. The remains of many ships that sank in storms or in battles rest at the bottom of the ocean. Part of the history of our civilizations lies waiting to be discovered. Perhaps there's even hidden treasure!